SCIENCE FACTS!

How to Talk to DOLPHINS

And Other Incredible Ideas About Animals

William Potter

Richard Watson

ARCTURUS

Arcturus

This edition published in 2025 by Arcturus Publishing Limited
26/27 Bickels Yard, 151-153 Bermondsey Street,
London SE1 3HA

Copyright © Arcturus Holdings Limited

All rights reserved. No part of this publication may be reproduced, stored in a retrieval system, or transmitted, in any form or by any means, electronic, mechanical, photocopying, recording or otherwise, without prior written permission in accordance with the provisions of the Copyright Act 1956 (as amended). Any person or persons who do any unauthorised act in relation to this publication may be liable to criminal prosecution and civil claims for damages.

Author: William Potter
Illustrator: Richard Watson
Consultants: Meriel Lland and Michael Leach
Designer: Sarah Fountain
Editor: Lydia Halliday
Design Manager: Rosie Bellwood-Moyler
Managing Editor: Joe Harris

ISBN: 978-1-3988-5055-2
CH011642US
Supplier 29, Date 0425, PI 00009059

Printed in China

Contents

Introduction to the Animal Kingdom	4
Weird and Wild	6
Chapter 1: Top Talents	7
How to Be Brainless	8
How to Change Color	10
How to Dodge the Dentist	12
Staying Snug	14
How to Sleep Upside Down	16
How to Breathe Underwater	18
How to Grow a New Arm	20
How to Be Sensitive	22
How to Cross the Desert	24
How to Leave Your Skin Behind	26
How to Live Forever	28
How to Fly like a Fish	30
Chapter 2: Chew on This!	31
How to Be a Team Player	32
How to Be a Bloodsucker	34
How to Eat Dinner Four Times	36
Super Senses	38
How to Feed a Whale	40
How to Eat Big	42
How to Headbang	44
How to Dine Like a Fly	46
How to Hunt with Bubbles	48
How to Be a Webmaster	50
How to See in the Dark	52
How to Live on Bamboo	54
Chapter 3: Meet the Family!	55
How to Be a Parent to Millions	56
How to Be a Clone	58
How to Sprout Wings	60
Showing Off	62
How to Never Grow Up	64

How to Pack a Pouch	66
How to Glow in the Dark	68
How to Be Irresistible	70
How to Talk to Dolphins	72
How to Look Your Best	74
How to Squeak in Silence	76
How to Sing Underwater	78
Chapter 4: Stay Sharp!	79
How to Inflate	80
How to Play Dead	82
Hide-and-Seek	84
How to Stun with a Sting	86
How to Fake a Snake	88
How to Hide in a Crowd	90
How to Grow Spiky Hair	92
How to Wear Your Skeleton	94
Keep Away!	96
How to Kick Up a Stink	98
How to Be a Squirt	100
How to Cause a Shock	102
Chapter 5: Home Sweet Home	103
How to Live in a Skyscraper	104
How to Build a Reef	106
How to Go Underground	108
How to Not Get Lost	110
How to Be a Popsicle	112
How to Walk on Ceilings	114
How to Mark Territory	116
Fast and Curious	118
How to Make a Giant Leap	120
How to Slime	122
How to Skip Winter	124
How to Be a Swing King	126
Index	128

Professor Albert Katzenstein's Introduction to the Animal Kingdom

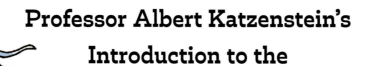

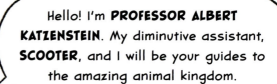

Hello! I'm **PROFESSOR ALBERT KATZENSTEIN**. My diminutive assistant, **SCOOTER**, and I will be your guides to the amazing animal kingdom.

If it's an **ANIMAL KINGDOM**, is there a king and queen?

We'll meet a **KINGFISHER** and a **QUEEN BEE**, so yes.

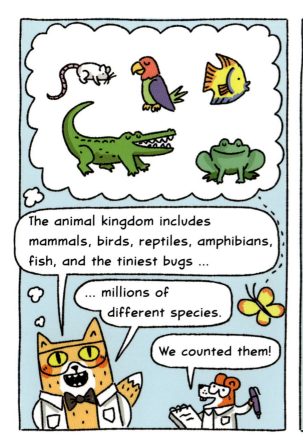

Top Talents
(Adapting to Survive)

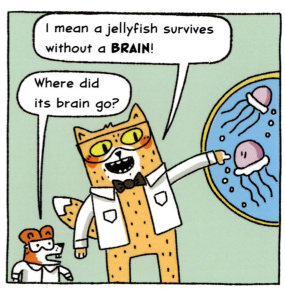

Jellyfish are not fish. Their correct name is **sea jellies**. These sea creatures do not have bones, a heart, lungs, blood ... or a **brain**.

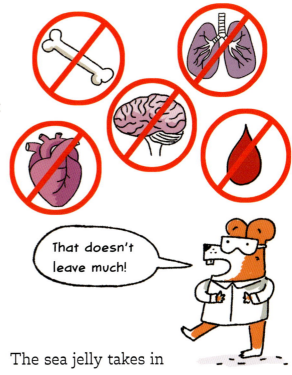

That doesn't leave much!

A sea jelly body is made up of a soft bell mostly filled with water. Sea jellies move by expanding and contracting this bell. Instead of a brain, a sea jelly senses its environment thanks to a **nerve net**, a series of nerves that send signals through its body.

The sea jelly takes in oxygen through the **epidermis** on the top of its bell, and this passes through its body without the need for lungs, a heart, or blood. Some jellies have simple eyes that can detect light. Inside the bell is the sea jelly's stomach. It takes in food and pushes out waste through a mouth below the bell.

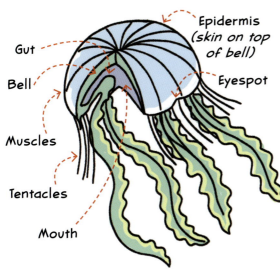

Below the bell is a series of stinging tentacles. These act as arms, bringing food toward the mouth.

So it doesn't have a **BOTTOM**, either!

I don't know what I'd do without my bottom!

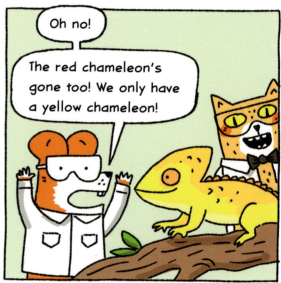

Chameleons are lizards with the amazing ability to change the color of their skin.

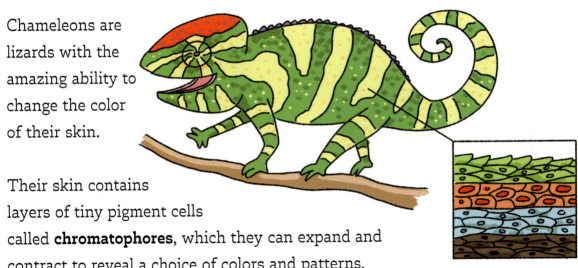

Their skin contains layers of tiny pigment cells called **chromatophores**, which they can expand and contract to reveal a choice of colors and patterns.

Do they change color for camouflage?

No, but a chameleon may blend into its surroundings with its natural green-brown color.

A chameleon changes color depending on its mood—if it's frightened or trying to communicate with another chameleon.

As well as their color changes, chameleons have eyes that can look in two different directions at the same time ...

... and the fastest tongue in nature.

Ugh, it has a **STICKY LICK!**

SLURP!

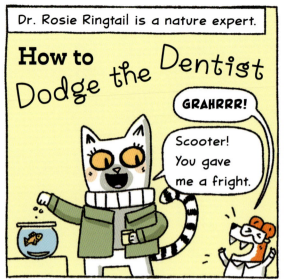

Sharks have different kinds of teeth depending on their diet, but all of them constantly replace their teeth. Behind the front rows are new teeth ready to more forward to replace the old ones that may break or fall out.

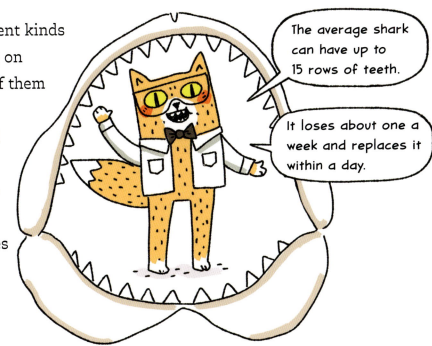

The average shark can have up to 15 rows of teeth.

It loses about one a week and replaces it within a day.

Do shark teeth get cavities?

No, because they are coated in **FLUORIDE**, an ingredient found in toothpaste ...

... and they don't eat candy!

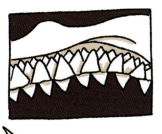

The front teeth of predatory sharks have slightly serrated edges, so they can cut through flesh. Sharks don't chew.

Sharks can get through 35,000 teeth in a lifetime!

I could do with a spare.

Staying Snug

Wild animals can't just turn on a radiator if they get cold. They have to rely on their bodies, coverings, or the environment to regulate their temperature.

Warm-blooded animals, such as mammals and birds, keep their body at a comfortable temperature by converting energy from food to heat and having an insulating coat of fur, feathers, or blubber.

Warm-blooded animals

Cold-blooded animals

Cold-blooded animals, such as lizards, fish, and insects, rely on their environment to keep them warm or cool. They may need to spend time basking in the sun or hiding in the shade.

Many warm-blooded animals that live around the poles, such as whales, seals, walruses, and penguins, have a thick layer of blubber as insulation, just under their skin. Blubber is fat which is a useful store of energy. It also helps keep the animals buoyant in the sea.

Large whales can have a layer of blubber more than 30 cm (12 in) thick!

Birds have feathers to keep them warm and aid them in flight. Their outer feathers lock together to form a barrier against wind and water.

The soft downy feathers of ducks and geese are used in bed covers and down jackets.

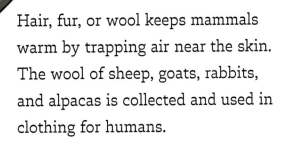

Hair, fur, or wool keeps mammals warm by trapping air near the skin. The wool of sheep, goats, rabbits, and alpacas is collected and used in clothing for humans.

Sleeping upside down from a ceiling might seem odd, but for bats, it's a smart idea. They are the only mammals that can fly, so staying on the roof of a cave ceiling or an old building keeps them out of reach of most predators. It also makes taking off easy—just drop and glide!

When hanging upside down, bats wrap their wings around them. They even hibernate in this position.

Not all bats sleep upside down. Some like to sleep in crevices.

Sloths spend about 60 percent of their lives hanging from a branch, asleep or barely moving. They digest food very slowly, taking up to 30 days to digest a leaf.

A sloth's internal organs are attached to its rib cage, so they don't press on its lungs when it is upside down, letting it breathe and snooze without problems.

17

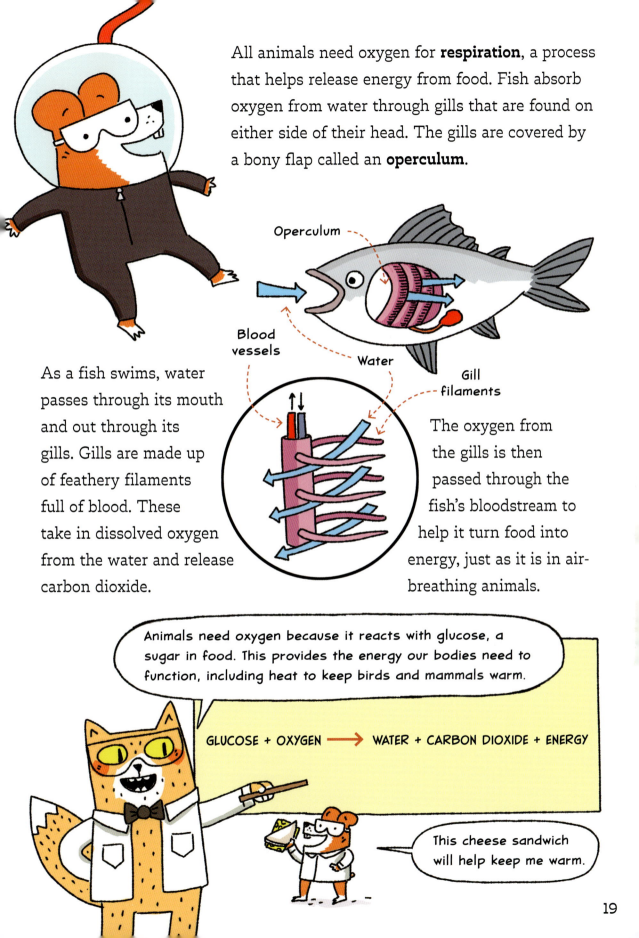

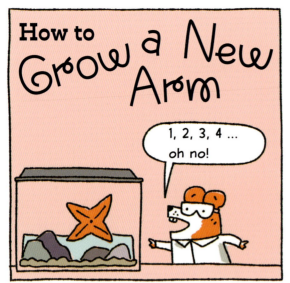

Starfish are not fish but **echinoderms**—marine animals without a backbone.

Starfish have five or more arms growing from a central body disk that contains a mouth.

When a starfish finds food (snails, mussels, and oysters), its arms pull open the shell, and the starfish pushes its stomach out through its mouth to eat the soft creature.

If a starfish loses an arm, it seals the wound, then begins building a new limb. It may take a year for the new arm to grow to full size.

Some starfish can grow their body back from a single arm, though they need some of their central disk. While they are growing their body back, they are said to be in their "comet form."

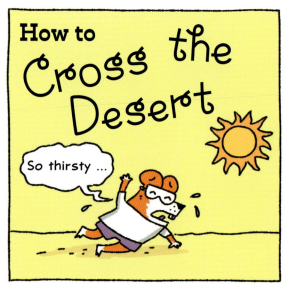

Camels are adapted for survival in the desert where there is little water.

When they can, they will gulp down gallons of water. Camels lose very little water through sweat and pee.

A camel's nose acts as a **humidifier**, cooling the air that it breathes out, so less water vapor is released.
Though camels are good at retaining water, they don't store it in their humps. The humps are fat reserves that provide energy, so camels can also survive without food on long journeys.

Even camel feet are adapted for the desert, with two wide toes on each foot that distribute their weight, keeping them from sinking deep into the sand.

Many animals **molt** or **shed skin** during their lives. Birds regularly lose feathers as they get worn and need replacing. Furry animals, like cats and dogs, shed hair in spring. They swap their thick "winter coat" for a thinner layer of fur, so they don't overheat in the warmer months.

Spiders, insects, and crustaceans have exoskeletons, tough shells that cannot expand as their bodies grow. They grow a new outer skin or shell and push themselves out of the old one. This is why you might find an empty crab shell on a beach.

Reptiles and amphibians shed their skin as they grow larger. Snakes shed their old, stretched skin by rubbing their head against a rock to split it. Then, they wriggle their way out in their new shiny skin, leaving the old skin behind.

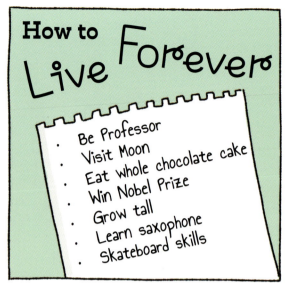

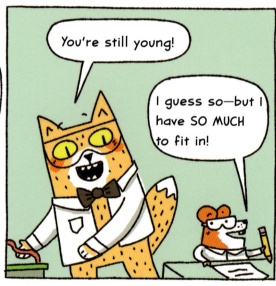

Jellyfish, or sea jellies, have an unusual lifecycle.

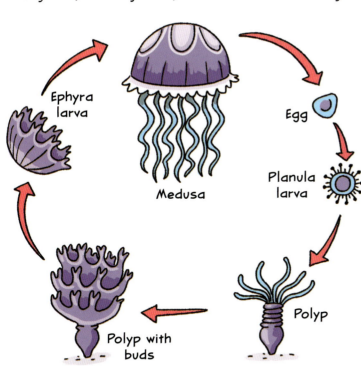

They are born from eggs as tiny **planula larvae** that float through the sea until they find a rock to latch on to.

Then, they transform into a **polyp**, a tentacled animal like an anemone, that collects food as it drifts by.

Polyps can duplicate themselves and build into a colony.

When the time is right, the polyps begin blooming like flowers, releasing **ephyra larvae**, or baby jellyfish. These develop into **medusae**, or adult jellyfish.

But, some jellyfish can reproduce by skipping stages. When the **immortal jellyfish** dies, its body sinks to the seabed and forms new polyps that turn into jellyfish in a form of **regeneration**.

Chew on This!

(Hunting and Feeding)

When it comes to hunting, some animals work as a team. **Wolves** live in family groups called **packs**. These are led by a dominant male and female.

"Who's the **LEADER** in our pack, Professor?"

"We're not a pack, Scooter ..."

"... but I think it's obvious."

By working together, wolves can hunt prey larger than themselves, such as deer and bison. Often, they will target a younger or injured animal.

As a team, they can track their prey, drive it away from its herd, and wear it out by taking turns chasing it. By attacking their prey from different angles, wolves make it harder for a lone animal to defend itself.

The wolves have roles, from chasing to attacking, and they know what to do by watching each other rather than by barking commands.

"Other animals that hunt as a team include lions, hyenas, wild dogs, chimpanzees, dolphins, and orca."

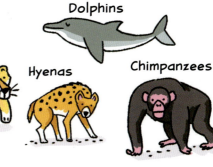

Lions

Hyenas

Dolphins

Chimpanzees

33

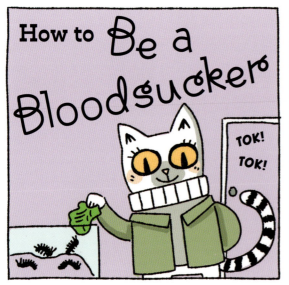

Vampire bats live in Mexico and Central and South America. Like most bats, they leave their roosts in caves, mines, or abandoned buildings after dark to feed, but they don't hunt for insects or fruit. They dine on blood.

Heat diagram of a goat

Vampire bats look for sleeping animals, such as goats, pigs, or cattle. They sneak up on them by crawling rather than flying. Heat sensors in their noses detect a warm spot on the animal, where blood is near the surface.

They give the animal a small cut with their sharp teeth, then they lap up the blood like milk. Vampire bats have a special chemical in their saliva (spit) that keeps the animal's blood from clotting, so the blood continues to flow until the bat has had its fill.

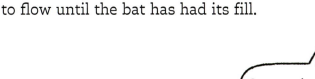

Does it hurt?

The animals often don't even wake up while the bat is feeding, but vampire bats can spread infections.

A vampire bat can drink about two tablespoons of blood during a 20-minute feed.

35

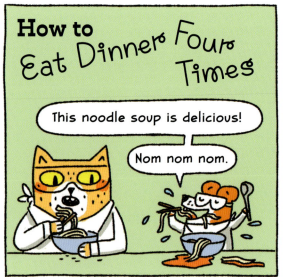

To get the best of the food they eat, some animals—called **ruminants**—digest their food more than once, using a series of separate stomachs.

To get nutrients from grass, cows have a stomach with four different chambers.

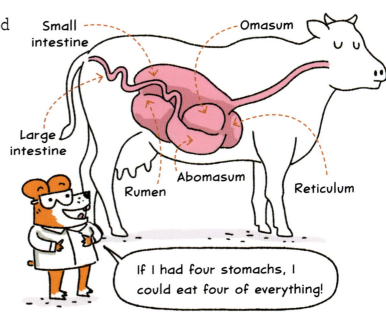

When a cow takes a bite of grass it only chews it a little before swallowing it. The grass then goes to the first and largest stomach chamber, the **rumen**.

A cow's rumen can hold up to 150 liters (40 gallons) of food material!

That even beats you, Scooter!

The food then passes to the small chamber—the **reticulum**—where it is mixed with saliva and turned to **cud**. This mushy mix is then pushed back up into the cow's mouth, so it can chew it some more.

The grass is broken down further in the **omasum** and the **abomasum**, where food is broken down by acids and substances called **enzymes**, which help with digestion.

Cows are not the only ruminants. Antelopes, deer, goats, sheep, and giraffes all have a four-chambered stomach to help them digest plants.

Super Senses

Infrared ← ---------- Visible spectrum ---------- → Ultraviolet

Sniff sniff! Someone's baking ... banana muffins!

You have a good sense of smell, Scooter, but some animals can smell, see, taste, and hear things that we can't.

The colors of the rainbow that we see form the visible spectrum, but beyond this are colors that our eyes can't make out. Birds can see **ultraviolet** colors, which appear as deep pinks, purples, and other bright shades.

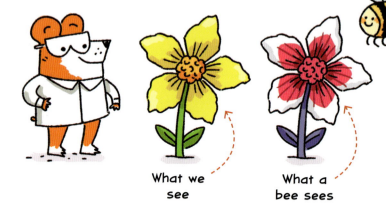

What we see

What a bee sees

Honeybees also see ultraviolet light along with blues and greens, so they see the patterns on flowers differently to us. These colors help lead bees to the flowers' nectar.

Beyond red on the visible spectrum is **infrared** radiation, produced by warm objects. Some species of snakes can detect this and locate prey in the dark.

Some animals can hear sounds that are too high or low-pitched for human ears to pick up. Bats use high-pitched **ultrasound** to help them understand their surroundings in the dark. Whales, elephants, and crocodiles communicate with low rumbling **infrasound**, which we cannot hear without special equipment. These deep sounds can travel for miles.

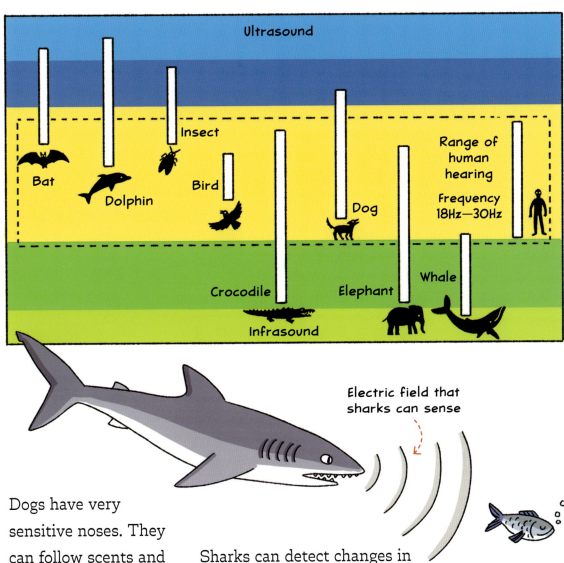

Dogs have very sensitive noses. They can follow scents and track animals and recognize the smell of an individual.

Sharks can detect changes in electric fields and locate fish by their movements. Sharks are also known for their ability to smell blood. It is thought that a shark could sniff out one drop of blood in the equivalent of a small swimming pool of water.

The **blue whale** is the largest animal that has ever lived on Earth, growing to 30 m (100 ft) in length and weighing up to 180 metric tons (200 tons).

A blue whale heart is the size of a small car!

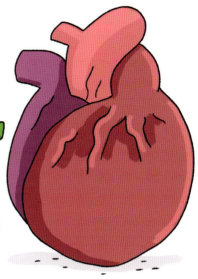

Despite its huge size, a blue whale eats some of the smallest sea creatures—krill.

Krill are crustaceans, like shrimp, that grow up to 6 cm (2.4 in) in length.

The blue whale is a filter feeder. Instead of teeth, it has brushlike structures called **baleen plates** attached to its upper jaw.

The whale swims through a swarm of krill with its mouth wide open. It then closes its mouth and pushes the water through its baleen plates to filter the water for krill, which it swallows. A blue whale will gobble up to 5 metric tons (5.5 tons) of krill each day.

Baleen plates

Tongue

A blue whale's tongue can weigh as much as an elephant!

Most snakes eat small prey, such as mice, birds, and worms, but some can swallow food even bigger than themselves. The Burmese python grows up to 5 m (16 ft) in length. It lives in jungles, swamps, and grasslands in Southeast Asia and has been known to eat pigs, deer, cows, and even alligators!

The python is a **constrictor**, and attacks prey by grabbing with its teeth, then wrapping its body around the animal and squeezing. Once the prey is unconscious, the python begins to swallow it whole.

A snake's jaws are loosely attached to its skull, joined by **ligaments** that enable it to open its jaws really wide. The snake uses backward-facing teeth to pull its body over its prey and into its stomach. It may take weeks to digest a huge meal, then the snake can go without food for months.

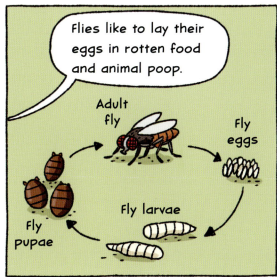

Humpback whales are social and highly intelligent creatures that can hunt in groups and use bubble nets to catch their prey.

When a pod of whales finds a school of fish, such as salmon or herring, they coordinate and dive below the fish. The whales swim in a circle blowing bubbles from the blowholes on their heads as they go.

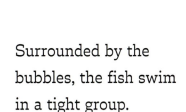

Surrounded by the bubbles, the fish swim in a tight group.

A lead whale will give a vocal signal, and the pod of whales swims upward at the same time with their mouths wide open. The whales then gulp down as many fish as they can fit in.

Dolphins have also been spotted using bubble nets to herd fish together.

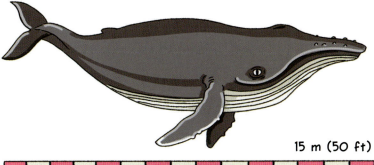

15 m (50 ft)

Humpback whales are huge, but they can't swallow any food larger than a grapefruit!

But I'm **SMALLER** than a grapefruit! Gulp!

49

Spider silk is one of the world's most incredible natural materials. It is used by spiders to form a sticky trap for prey, as a nest, and for weaving a protective cocoon for their young.

The silk is made in the spider's body and released as a liquid through its **spinneret**. The spider guides the silk out with its legs, and the silk hardens to form threads.

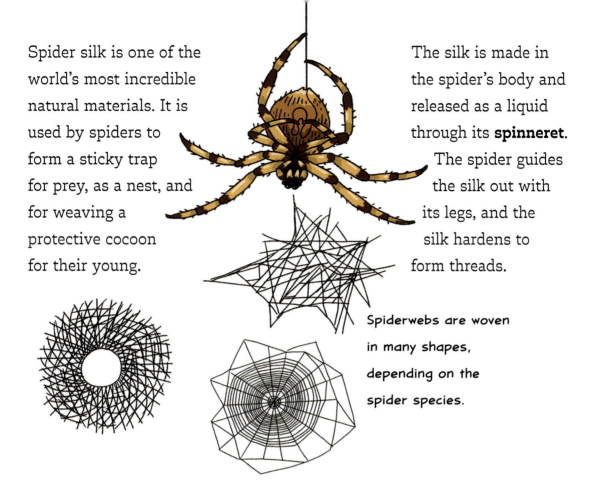

Spiderwebs are woven in many shapes, depending on the spider species.

When an insect is caught in the sticky silk, the spider feels the vibrations as the prey tries to escape. It hurries over to bite and inject venom that kills its prey. Then it wraps it in more silk to eat later.

Spider silk is stronger than steel with the same diameter, yet very stretchy.

Spider silk is so amazing that scientists have been trying to create an artificial version.

How long will I be stuck here?

51

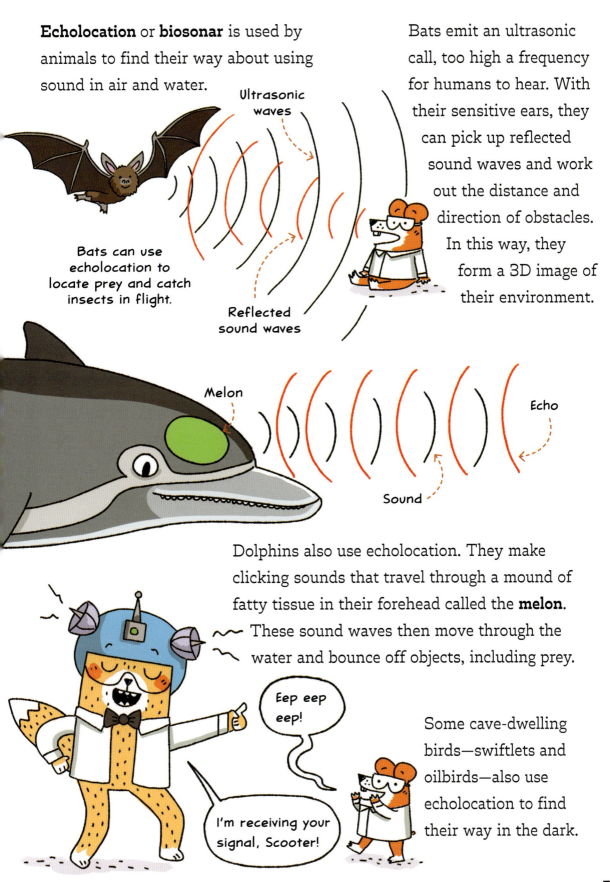

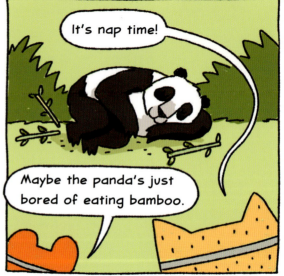

Meet the Family!
(Development, Social Life, Communication)

Sunfish are large flattened fish that can grow to be about 1.8 m (6 ft) across.

Their size deters most predators. Sunfish eat jellyfish, squid, and small fish. Matching their name, sunfish have a habit of lying flat on the water's surface to soak in the sun.

Female ocean sunfish carry more eggs than any other known animal with a backbone—an estimated 300 million! Rather than having a few babies and caring for them, sunfish release a lot of eggs and leave them at risk of being eaten by other animals. But with 300 million young floating about, there is a good chance of many surviving.

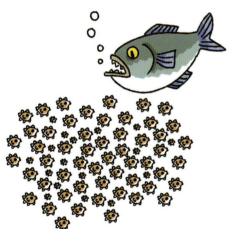

The fry swim in schools for protection until they are large enough to survive on their own. Those that survive to adulthood can end up 60 million times heavier than their original weight of 1 g (0.04 oz).

Cloning means using an organism's cells to make a new creature that is genetically identical to it. While scientists have been creating clones for decades, it's been happening in the natural world for millions of years. **Aphids** are insects that give birth to clones.

Aphids can reproduce at an incredible rate. Female aphids are born pregnant and give birth to young that are clones of themselves. The females live for about 25 days and can give birth to about 80 new aphids. The young are all pregnant females, too, and can give birth within days. In this way, a colony of thousands of aphids can spring up in just weeks!

Aphids feed on the sap (dissolved sugars and minerals) of a plant's new growth, which can affect a plant's health.

When the aphid colony's host plant becomes crowded, some aphids are born with wings, so they can fly away to start a new colony on a different plant.

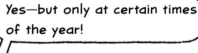

Some generations of aphids include both males *and* females. When this happens, the insects mate with each other. The females lay eggs rather than giving birth to live young. Those eggs all hatch as females ... and the cycle begins again.

59

Metamorphosis is a dramatic change that takes place in an animal's body structure. Rather than growing from tiny versions of adults, they start life in one form, then transform into another midway through their life.

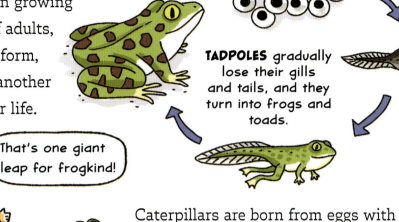

TADPOLES gradually lose their gills and tails, and they turn into frogs and toads.

That's one giant leap for frogkind!

DRAGONFLIES change from a waterborne nymph into a winged dragonfly.

Caterpillars are born from eggs with a single mission—to eat. This is their **larva** stage. Caterpillars quickly gain weight and **molt** several times as their body expands. But, inside their body are groups of cells waiting to develop into the body parts of an adult butterfly or moth.

CATERPILLARS transform into butterflies and moths.

When the caterpillar reaches a certain size, it attaches itself to a leaf. Most butterfly caterpillars form a hard shell called a **chrysalis**. Moth caterpillars may spin a silk **cocoon**. This is their **pupa** stage. Inside, their body turns into a soup of cells that come together to build an adult body with legs, wings, and antennae.

Once complete, the adult butterfly or moth emerges, stretches, and dries its wings, then flies free.

I'm a Scooterfly!

JELLYFISH change from polyps to tentacled sea jellies.

Showing Off

Many male animals go through courtship displays to attract females. This might involve singing, a dance, or displays of color.

Male birds usually have more colorful or longer feathers than females, and they proudly display them, sometimes raising or waving them to attract a mate. One of the most famous bird displays is that of the peacock with its impressive fan of raised tail feathers.

Some birds, like the bird-of-paradise and grouse, do an elaborate dance, call, or sing to draw the attention of females.

Males may offer gifts for females. The male bowerbird collects brightly colored objects, usually blue, and displays them to attract a female. Kingfishers offer fish to potential mates.

In the amphibian world, frogs attract mates through their loud croaking calls, while newts may perform a series of back-and-forth movements. In some cases, both male and female animals perform a series of moves together.

The great crested grebe is a waterbird that dances in an elaborate duet. Pairs lift themselves out of the water and offer pondweed to each other in a series of synchronized actions.

Grebes performing courtship dance with pondweed

For some animals, courtship is a matter of life and death. Male spiders are often much smaller than the female and may seem like a handy snack. They must approach the female carefully, with a series of signals to show that they are a mate, not dinner.

The courtship displays are an effort by the male to show off his beauty, fitness, and ability to find food and build nests for a potential partner. The male may face competition to impress, with several males performing at the same time.

The male peacock spider attracts a mate with a colorful display, dance, and vibrations.

63

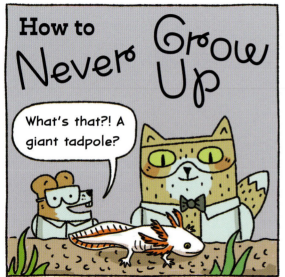

Axolotls are amphibians that grow into adults without going through **metamorphosis**. They are native to freshwater ponds in Mexico and feed on mollusks, worms, and insects.

Axolotls are **neotenic**, which means they keep their juvenile features. While frogs and newts lose their tail and gills when they change from tadpoles into adults, axolotls stay looking like a large tadpole. They keep a finned tail, weak limbs, no eyelids, and external, feathery gills, unlike regular salamanders ...

Though other adult amphibians spend most of their life in damp conditions on land, axolotls cannot easily take oxygen from the air, so they avoid leaving the water for more than a few minutes.

Adult salamander

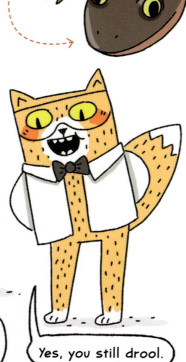

I guess I haven't changed that much since I was a baby either.

Yes, you still drool.

As well as retaining their youthful features, axolotls can regenerate parts of their body if lost or injured. If they lose a limb, tail, or even part of their eye, heart, or brain, they can grow it back over a period of months.

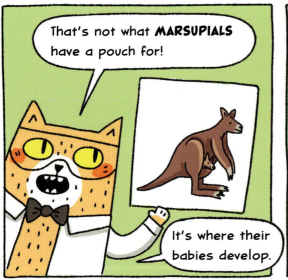

Marsupials are mammals that produce immature young. Their newborn babies, called **joeys**, are tiny, helpless, furless, and blind. A kangaroo joey is just 2.5 cm (1 in) long when born.

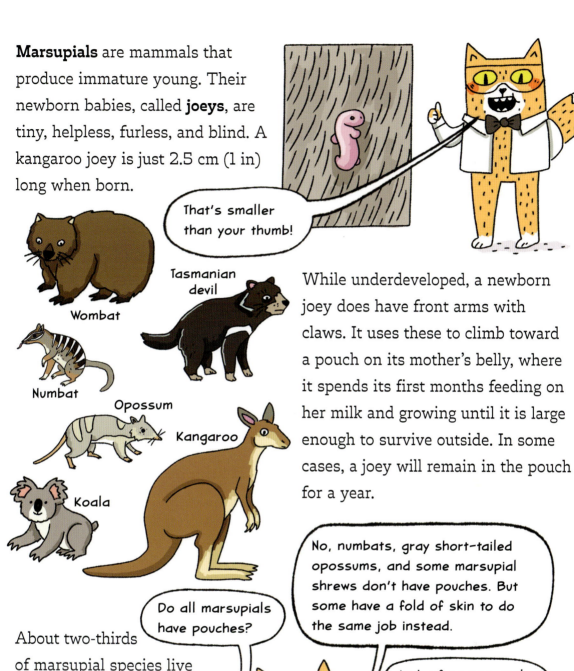

That's smaller than your thumb!

Wombat

Tasmanian devil

Numbat

Opossum

Kangaroo

Koala

While underdeveloped, a newborn joey does have front arms with claws. It uses these to climb toward a pouch on its mother's belly, where it spends its first months feeding on her milk and growing until it is large enough to survive outside. In some cases, a joey will remain in the pouch for a year.

About two-thirds of marsupial species live in Australasia, with various species of opossums found in the Americas.

Marsupials include the kangaroo, koala, wombat, Tasmanian devil, and opossum.

Do all marsupials have pouches?

No, numbats, gray short-tailed opossums, and some marsupial shrews don't have pouches. But some have a fold of skin to do the same job instead.

And, of course, male marsupials don't have pouches.*

So, the women do all the baby-carrying. Typical!

*The water opossum is the only exception.

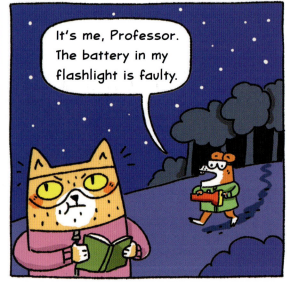

Some animals can make their own light, which they use to communicate, attract mates, or to hunt in the dark. This process is called **bioluminescence**. Bioluminescence works through a chemical reaction within the animal's body.

Fireflies (also known as lightning bugs) are a kind of beetle that can use bioluminescence to send signals to other fireflies.

Firefly

Some female bugs glow to mimic other species, attracting male beetles, so they can eat them!

That's super-sneaky!

In the ocean, several animal species communicate with lights, including **jellyfish**, **comb jellies**, and **shrimp**, which use lights to attract prey or to startle predators.

Cave-dwelling **fungus gnats** also use bioluminescence to catch prey by dangling sticky webs around their glowing light. The light attracts moths that get caught in the trap.

Yikes! What a light-up fright!

Anglerfish

The **anglerfish** has a light-up lure sprouting from its head. When a tasty fish comes closer to investigate the light, the anglerfish grabs it with its long fangs.

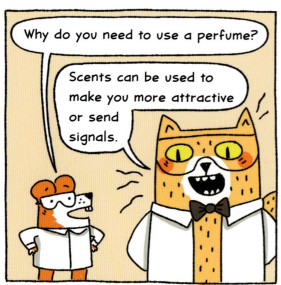

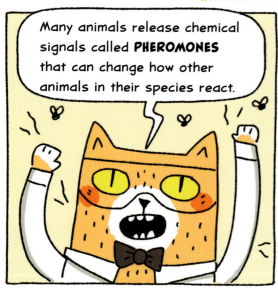

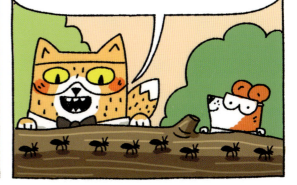

Dolphins are very intelligent and communicate with each other using clicks, whistles, and loud pulses, as well as through touch and movement.

Scientists have found ways to communicate with dolphins, too! They have tried to find patterns in their sounds and attempted to share messages with dolphins.

Dolphins can be trained to do tasks and make sounds and gestures to humans when they want food or for a game to continue.

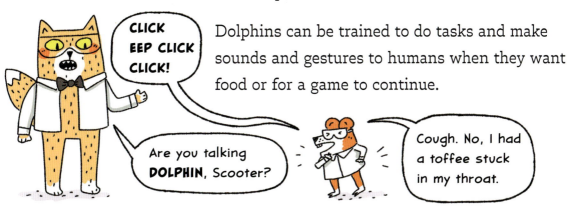

While animals use sounds to communicate, it is thought that they do not have complex languages like humans. Apes, such as chimpanzees, can alert each other to danger through sounds. The sounds they make can even identify a specific threat.

Even though we recognize that animals communicate through sound and other means, we are not yet able to copy it.

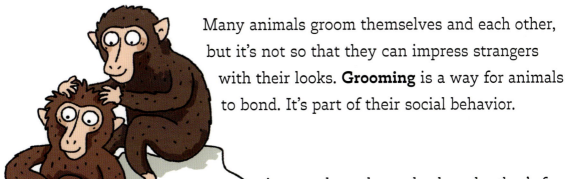

Many animals groom themselves and each other, but it's not so that they can impress strangers with their looks. **Grooming** is a way for animals to bond. It's part of their social behavior.

Apes and monkeys check each other's fur for parasites, dirt, and dead skin. They can help clean hard-to-reach spots. Grooming helps keep an animal clean and healthy, but it also helps them form bonds such as friendships. If one animal grooms another, it may later be rewarded with food or protection.

Grooming can make an animal feel calmer by causing them to produce chemicals in the brain called **endorphins**, which make the animal feel better.

Apes and monkeys are not the only animals that groom each other to improve their social bonds. Horses, deer, lions, meerkats, birds, and bats also do it with members of the same species. Cattle will often lick each other as part of their grooming.

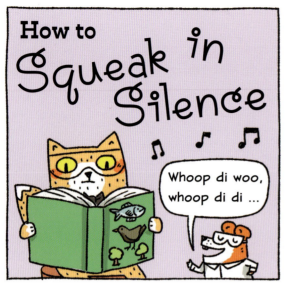

Tarsiers are tiny nocturnal primates that were once thought to be silent. Then, it was discovered that they squeak to each other using **ultrasound**, noises that are at a frequency too high for humans to hear, even higher than a dog whistle.

Tarsier ears are specially adapted to receive their high-frequency squeaks and work out which direction they are coming from. Not only do the squeaks enable a tarsier to spread an alarm when predators are near, the squeaks are at too high a frequency for predators to hear, so they do not give away the tarsier's position.

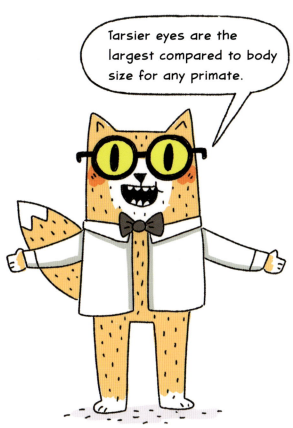

Tarsier eyes are the largest compared to body size for any primate.

Large eyes enable the tarsier to receive a lot of light, so it can hunt after dark. Sensitive ears help it locate crickets and cockroaches in the bush by their quiet movements. With its long legs, the tarsier can leap from tree to tree to grab a bug in its long, skinny fingers.

Stay Sharp!
(Avoiding Predators)

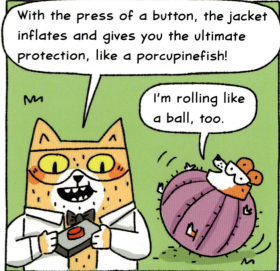

Porcupinefish have a clever way of putting off predators—they swell up like a spiky balloon.

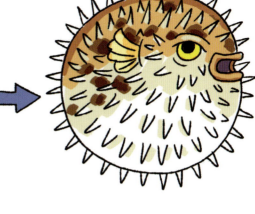

By quickly swallowing water or air, they can swell up to almost twice their size when relaxed. They also have sharp spines, like a porcupine, and these spring up when they are inflated, making them a doubly difficult dish to dine on.

Porcupinefish are served as a delicacy in some restaurants, but chefs have to train for years to deal with them since the fish contain a **deadly poison** called **tetrodotoxin** in their skin and internal organs.

Because of their special defenses, porcupinefish can feel relatively safe swimming slowly near reefs. Their teeth form a tough parrotlike beak that they use to crack open hard-shelled animals such as snails and clams.

Does anything eat porcupine fish, then?

Sharks and orcas sometimes eat them, and humans, too, but they have to be very, very careful ...

Another fish that can inflate its body to a great size as a defense is the **pufferfish**, which doesn't have spines like the porcupinefish.

pufferfish

81

"**Playing possum**" means pretending to be dead. It comes from the behavior of the North American **Virginia opossum** when it is threatened by predators. The opossum lies perfectly still on the ground with its eyes closed, mouth open, and tongue sticking out.

It may also poop to make the act more convincing.

I'm convinced!

Opossum

The trick works because most predators only hunt live prey. A predator may think that the animal is ill or poisoned, and so it's not a safe meal to touch.

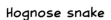

Hognose snake

Eek! A snake! Tell me when it's gone!

The opposum is not the only animal that does this trick. The **hognose snake** will lie with its mouth open and release a foul-smelling liquid that makes it seem like it's rotting!

A fish called the **sleeper cichlid** pretends to play dead to catch other fish. It lies flat on the bottom of a lake, and its skin turns blotchy. When another fish investigates, the cichlid wakes up and grabs it.

Sleeper cichlid

Hide-and-Seek

Camouflage is the use of patterns and shades to blend into the background. Animals benefit from this because it keeps them hidden from predators and also enables them to sneak up on their own prey.

Many lizards, amphibians, and insects have developed green or brown colors, so they are harder to see in leafy environments. Some creatures take it to the next level by growing bodies that resemble leaves, twigs, and flowers.

When it stays still, the **stick insect** is almost impossible to spot among twigs. It even sways to imitate a branch in a breeze. **Leaf insects** are related to stick insects, but they have flattened bodies shaped like foliage.

Female **thorn bugs** grow enlarged, pointed thoraxes (middle body sections) which let them hide on a thorny plant while they feed on its sap.

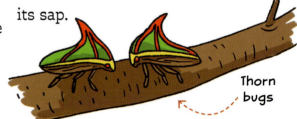

Thorn bugs

Nightjars and **owls** are birds with feathers with patterns that blend into the markings on tree bark.

Underwater, the **stonefish** has a mottled pattern that looks like the reefs and rocks that it rests on. It even has seaweed growing on it. This sneaky predator ambushes prey that happen to swim too close.

Animals that live in the far north change their camouflage during the winter months. In summer, the Arctic fox, hare, weasel, and ptarmigan all have brown or gray fur or feathers that hide them among plants and rocks. When snow begins to fall, they lose their dark fur and replace it with a white winter coat.

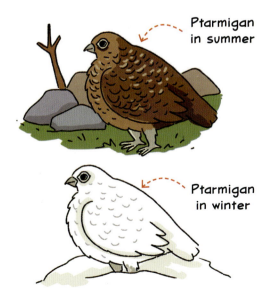

Ptarmigan in summer

Ptarmigan in winter

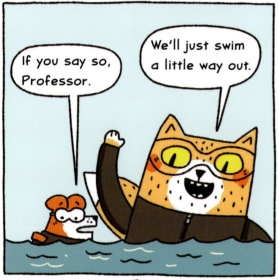

Jellyfish float near the ocean surface. They rely on food coming to them, within reach of their tentacles.

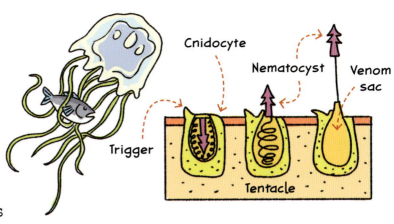

On each tentacle, the jellyfish carries a series of stinging cells called **cnidocytes**. These stun prey, so it can be pulled up toward the jellyfish's mouth.

The cnidocytes are cells of venom with a tiny trigger. When prey, such as a small fish, swims against the trigger, the cell opens and lets in seawater. This causes a needlelike tube called a **nematocyst** to shoot out and inject the prey with venom in a fraction of a second.

The **box jellyfish** delivers a venom that can affect a human heart. Anyone stung by one must seek medical assistance immediately. Many governments give warnings where box jellyfish are common.

87

Mimicry is one of nature's greatest tricks. To avoid becoming prey, some animals pretend to be a completely different creature, one less tasty or more frightening.

Hoverfly

Some animals grow to resemble bad-tasting creatures. They confuse predators that believe them to be their inedible look-alike. The harmless **hoverfly** deters birds by displaying colors and patterns that match the stinging **hornet**.

When it begins life, the **spicebush swallowtail caterpillar** puts off potential predators by resembling a bird dropping. As it grows, yellow rings with black spots develop on its head. If a bird gets close, the caterpillar dips its head, so it looks like a threatening snake.

Spicebush swallowtail caterpillar

To avoid getting eaten, the **mimic octopus** can wiggle its body into different shapes to imitate the look and movements of jellyfish, sea snakes, and highly venomous **lionfish**.

89

Porcupines are rodents that live in parts of the Americas, Asia, Europe, and Africa. They usually rest in burrows or rocky crevices during the day and forage for food after dark.

Porcupines have a special way of keeping predators at bay. They grow long spines and sharp **quills** over their back. The quills are modified hairs coated with **keratin**, the same material found in human fingernails and animal horns. They can grow up to 30 cm (12 in) in length.

If threatened by a lion or hyena, for example, the porcupine raises its quills and turns to point them toward the danger. The porcupine may shake its quills together to make a rattling warning sound.

Porcupines may push their quills into an animal that threatens them. The quill can injure the attacker and lead to infection. Just like hairs, the porcupine can grow and replace lost quills.

Turtles, tortoises, and terrapins are reptiles and the only vertebrates (animals with backbones) to have an external shell. The shells protect their soft bodies from predators and the weather.

The shell is joined to a turtle's skeleton and made up of a domed carapace over the top of the body and a flatter plastron under the belly. The shell develops from flattened ribs.

A turtle shell is made of about 60 bones with an outer layer of scutes, or scales, made of keratin, a material that makes animal hair and horn. Land-dwelling turtles tend to have a domed shell. Sea-dwelling turtles have flatter and smoother shells to make it easier for them to swim.

If threatened, most turtles can withdraw their head and legs inside the tough shell.

Keep Away!

Many animals use alarm calls to warn of danger, but some also make noises to scare other animals away.

A **rattlesnake** alerts approaching predators by tightening muscles in its tail, then shaking the segmented scales at the end to make a rattling sound.

A male **mountain gorilla** will stand upright, then beat his chest and roar if a male rival comes too close to his family. If the rival doesn't move away, the gorilla may charge and fight.

Poison dart frogs may look handsome in bright shades of yellow, orange, and blue, but these are warning colors meant to tell other animals that eating them will be very unpleasant, if not fatal.

The toxic **fire salamander** also displays warning shades. Reptiles, such as snakes, and many insects use bright colors and patterns to alert potential predators that they are dangerous to approach or harmful if eaten.

The **lionfish** boasts bright red and white stripes to remind other fish that it carries venom in its spines. The **blue-ringed octopus** has a pattern with a very clear message—it is highly venomous.

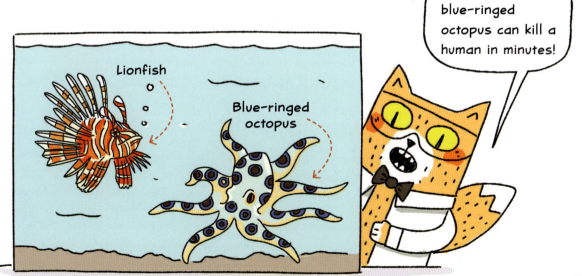

A bite from a blue-ringed octopus can kill a human in minutes!

Striped skunk

The **striped skunk** is a North American mammal with a potent way of warding off potential attackers. It has scent glands on its rear and these can spray one of the most unpleasant smells in the animal kingdom.

Skunks eat mostly insects and have few natural predators, who know to avoid them. If bothered by a mountain lion, coyote, fox, or bird of prey, the skunk raises its tail and sprays a noxious chemical. The spray can reach several meters. As well as delivering a lingering nasty stink, the spray can cause a burning sensation in the eyes.

Other animals that spray to keep predators away include the **bombardier beetle** which fires burning chemicals from its rear. The **Texas horned lizard** squirts blood from the corners of its eyes. The blood is mixed with a nasty-tasting chemical, too.

Bombardier beetle

99

Cephalopods, including **squid**, **octopuses**, and **cuttlefish**, can release a cloud of ink into the water when they are threatened.

The ink is produced in sacs between the cephalopod's gills. When approached, the creature squirts out a thick cloud of dark ink from its bottom and uses it for cover while it swims away from the confused predator.

Some clever cephalopods squirt ink in shapes that look like dark copies of themselves, so the predator chases after them instead. The cuttlefish is known to cover its eggs in ink, perhaps to hide them.

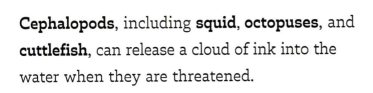

My latest masterpiece!

Cuttlefish

Cuttlefish eggs

Stop wriggling!

The ink is mostly made of **melanin**, the natural chemical that gives color to human skin, hair, and eyes. Squid ink was once used in writing tools and is also used as an ingredient in some rice and pasta dishes.

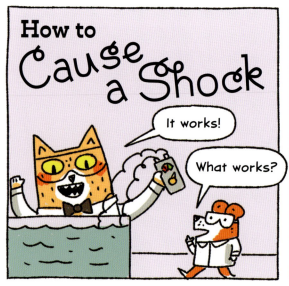

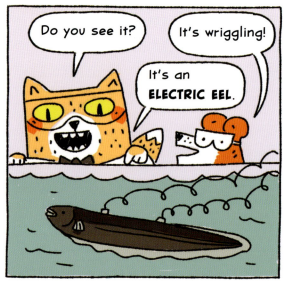
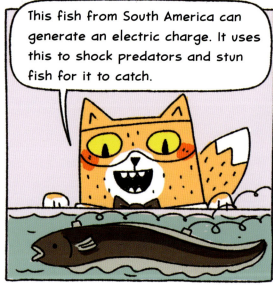

Home Sweet Home

(Homes, Environments)

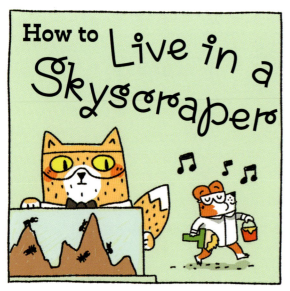

Across parts of Africa, Australia, and South America, tall structures up to 5 m (17 ft) high can be seen in the landscape. These are the homes of **termites**, small insects that live in huge colonies.

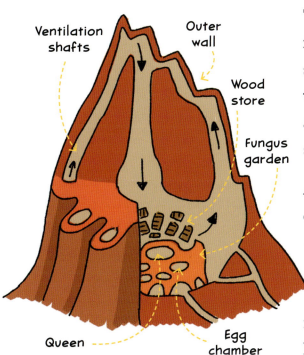

The towering termite mounds are built from a mix of soil, dung, and termite spit. Inside the mounds are shafts and tunnels that provide pathways and airflow to keep the mound at a steady temperature.

At the heart of the nest is the **termite queen**, which lays about 30,000 eggs a day for the colony. She is cared for by blind and wingless worker termites who also tend to her young in a nursery. The colony is guarded by larger, biting soldier termites.

The termites eat plants and wood. Chewed plant matter is used to feed fungus inside the mound as a food source for the colony.

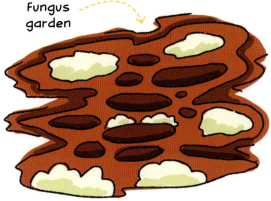

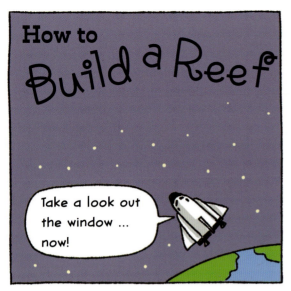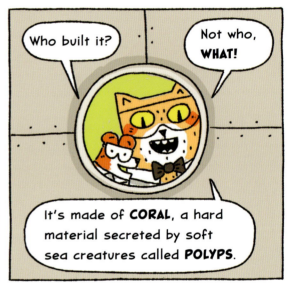

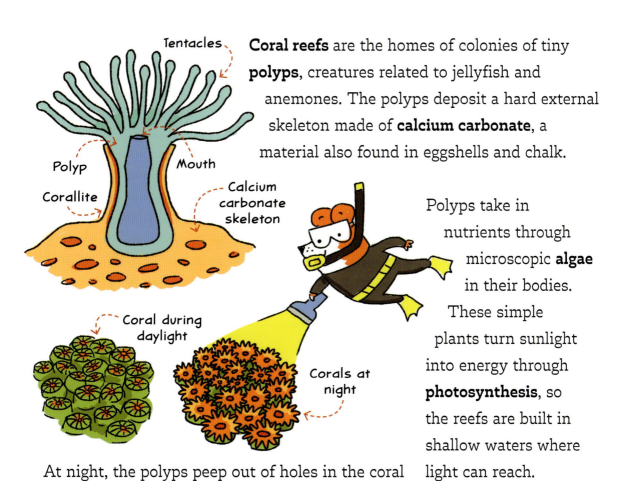

Coral reefs are the homes of colonies of tiny **polyps**, creatures related to jellyfish and anemones. The polyps deposit a hard external skeleton made of **calcium carbonate**, a material also found in eggshells and chalk.

Polyps take in nutrients through microscopic **algae** in their bodies. These simple plants turn sunlight into energy through **photosynthesis**, so the reefs are built in shallow waters where light can reach.

At night, the polyps peep out of holes in the coral and use their tentacles to collect passing food.

The coral skeletons built by polyps can take many shapes, from wide fans, tubes, and branches to domes and cabbage-like forms. Reefs become the shelter and feeding grounds for many different sea creatures.

107

Animals live underground for various reasons. Burrows provide an escape from large predators, shelter from the weather, and a safe place for rearing young.

Animals that dig their own burrows are called **primary excavators**. These animals include the **armadillo**, **mole**, **rabbit**, and **wombat**, all of which have strong front claws.

A **rabbit** warren can be home for a family of 60 animals, with nesting chambers for kittens and larders of food. A network of **prairie dog** burrows can extend for hundreds of acres.

Some animals claim the burrows dug by others as their own and make changes. These are called **secondary modifiers**.

Badgers and **armadillos** only come out of their burrows after dark, when it's safer to look for food. Some animals, such as the **mole**, spend almost all their lives beneath ground, digging through the earth in search of insects, worms, and roots.

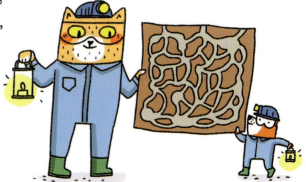

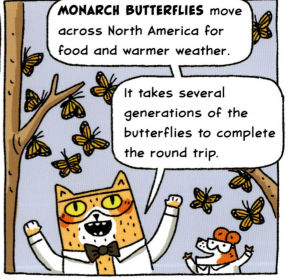

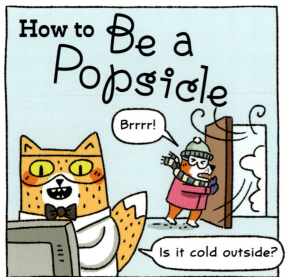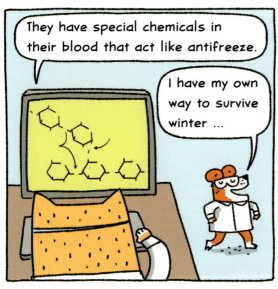

Animals deal with the cold in different ways. Some migrate, some hibernate, some grow furry or blubbery coats. Then there are those that freeze.

When the temperature drops, the North American **wood frog** finds a cozy pile of leaves and lets the cold take over. Its heart, breathing, and brain activity slow down and come to a stop, but it doesn't die.

The frog survives because it pumps out much of its body's water and replaces it with thick chemicals called **cryoprotectants** that work like antifreeze.

The frog can survive for up to eight months through temperatures as low as −14 °C (7 °F). When the weather warms up, the frog defrosts and hops back to life.

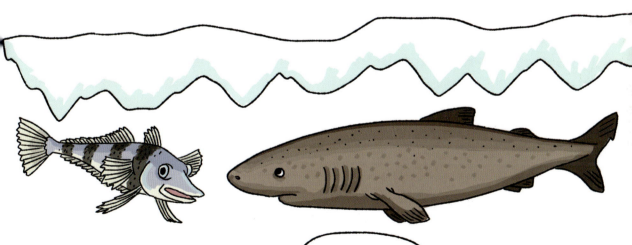

Other animals with "antifreeze" in their body include the white-blooded **icefish** and the **Greenland shark**, which swim below the ice around the poles.

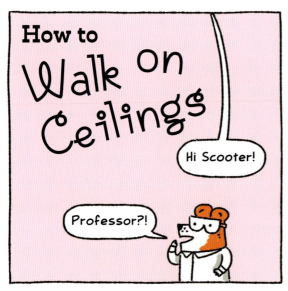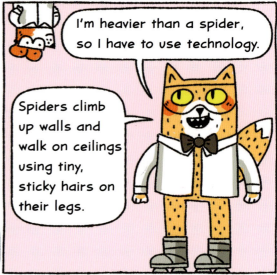

Spiders, **ants**, and **geckos** can walk up walls and across ceilings. This is due to tiny hairs on their feet and the fact that they are very light, so gravity has less of a pull on them.

Even the hairs on spider feet have hairs, microscopic bristles called **spatulae** that can fit into the smallest holes in what may look like a smooth surface. They take advantage of a property known as **Van der Waals force**.

Geckos and tree frogs can walk up vertical surfaces due to the tiny hairs spread over their wide toes.

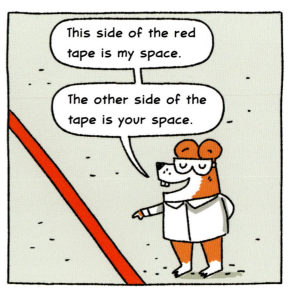

Not every animal is happy to share space. Some protect their area fiercely, in order to guard their food and water sources, and to deter rivals from trying to claim mates or control their group.

Animals will usually have a **home range** that they regularly visit. To let other animals know that they are around, animals may leave **scent markings**.

When animals spray, they may also secrete special scents from glands, which can also indicate that they are looking for a mate. Bears and lemurs have scent glands on their paws or arms. Deer have them between their eyes, antlers, and on their feet.

Wolves, frogs, and birds announce their territory through song or **vocal marking**. If a rival ignores the calls, it may be attacked.

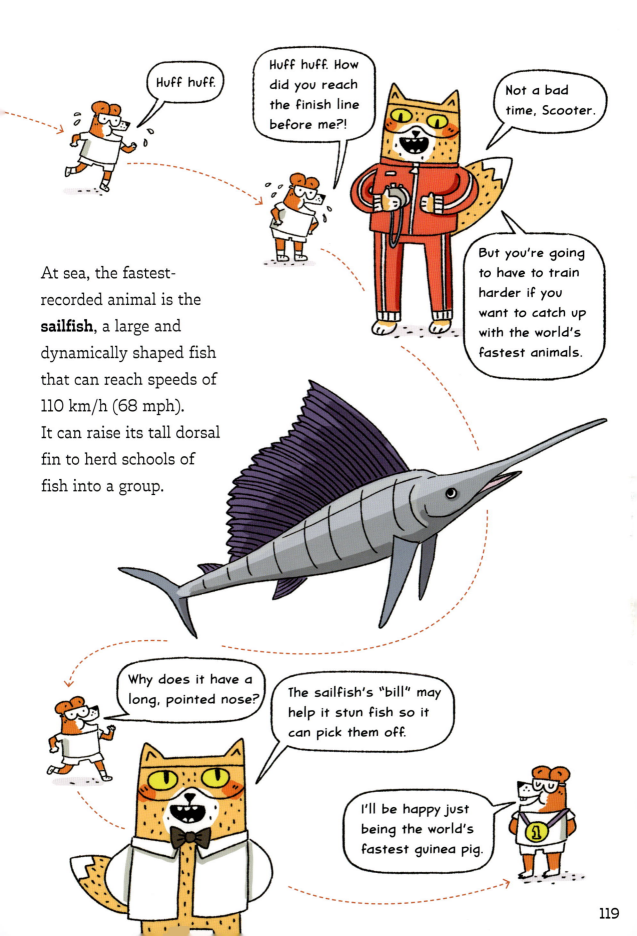

The **flea** is a tiny flightless insect that feeds on the blood of mammals and birds. It grows to just 3 mm (0.13 in) in length.

Though they don't have wings, fleas can take to the air, thanks to extremely long and powerful back legs that enable them to leap 130 times their body length.

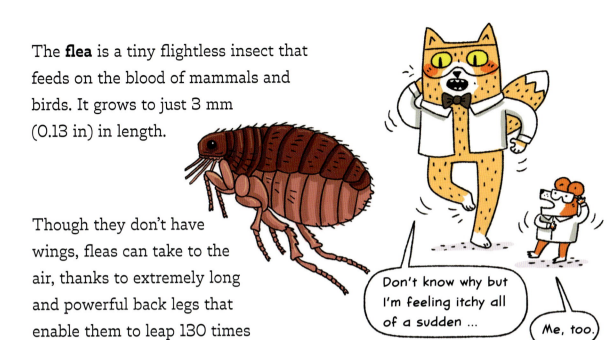

Don't know why but I'm feeling itchy all of a sudden ...

Me, too.

That's equivalent to a human jumping over the Eiffel Tower!

Before a leap, they store their muscle energy in blocks of a substance called **resilin**, before releasing it in one mighty spring like a bow firing an arrow.

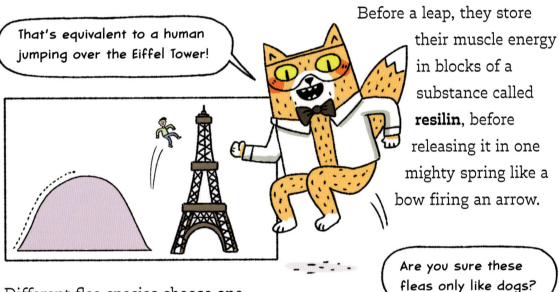

Different flea species choose one type of animal to be their host. Once they find it, they cling on with their sharp claws, then pierce the animal's skin and suck on its blood. Fleas lay their tiny white eggs on the host, too. Unless the fleas and eggs are removed, the host animal can soon have a serious flea problem.

Are you sure these fleas only like dogs?

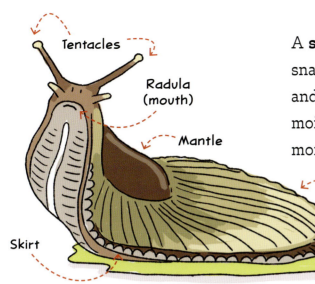

A **slug** is a land **gastropod**, like a snail but without a shell. Both slugs and snails need to keep their skin moist, but without a shell, slugs have more of a problem with drying out.

To survive, slugs spend most of their time in damp places and come out after rain or at night. They also secrete a protective **mucus** to keep them moist.

Mucus is secreted by the foot and left behind by slugs and snails as a slimy trail. This slime helps them glide over rough or dry surfaces and also helps them find a mate.

Other animals that secrete mucus include the **parrotfish** and the **hagfish**. The parrotfish creates a cocoon of mucus for it to sleep inside at night. The eel-like hagfish can produce a bucketful of slime in an instant by mixing it with seawater.

Winter can be a hard time for wild animals. There is less food available, and the ground may be covered in snow. To survive the coldest months, some animals choose to sit it out by **hibernating**. Animals that hibernate include bears, bats, hedgehogs, and many small rodents.

Hibernators find a safe place to shelter. Bears dig a den. Hedgehogs nestle in a pile of leaves. Rodents may make a nest of dry grass in a burrow. Small animals store food in their dens. Bears fill themselves up with as much food as they can to build up fat reserves, since they won't be eating again for months.

As the weather cools, the hibernating animal's heart rate, breathing, and body temperature drop dramatically. It can stay in this state of **torpor** for months. When the weather warms up, the animal slowly revives and is ready to forage for food again.

125

Primates (apes and monkeys) can swing between tree branches using just their arms. This is called **brachiation**.

Orangutans brachiate, but the true experts are **spider monkeys** and **gibbons**. With arms longer than their legs, they can swing between vines and branches with ease. To aid them in brachiation, these primates have short spines, flexible wrists that mean they can twist between swings, and long fingers with nails instead of claws for maintaining a good grip.

Using brachiation and huge leaps, gibbons can cross the jungle at up to 56 km/h (35 mph). Humans can also brachiate, though not at the same level as a gibbon. Monkey bars in playgrounds are a good place to practice.

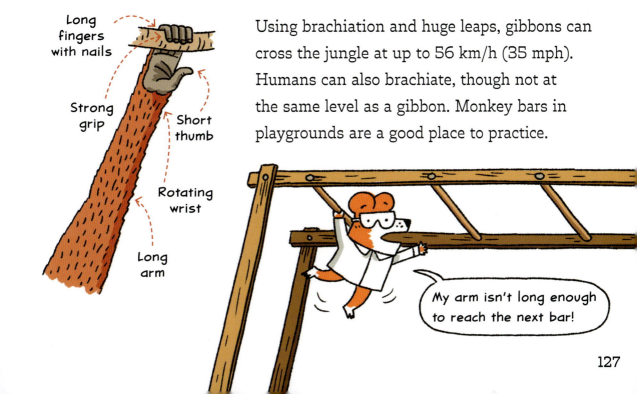

Index

Ant 71, 115
Aphid 59
Axolotl 64–65
Bat 16-17, 34-35, 39, 52-53, 125
Bear 14, 117, 124–125
Bee 38, 71
Bioluminescence 68–69
Brachiation 127
Burrowing 108–109
Butterfly 61, 110
Camel 24–25
Camouflage 11, 84–85, 90–91
Caterpillar 61, 89
Chameleon 10–11
Cheetah 118
Chimpanzee 33, 73
Cloning 58–59
Cocoon 60–61
Coral 106–107
Courtship 62–63
Cow 37, 43, 75
Desert 24–25
Dolphin 33, 39, 49, 53, 72–73
Echinoderm 21
Echolocation 52–53
Electric eel 102
Exoskeleton 27
Firefly 68–69
Flea 120–121
Fly 46–47, 89
Flying fish 30
Frog 14, 27, 61, 63, 65, 97, 113, 115, 117
Gecko 115
Gills 18-19, 65, 101
Grooming 74–75
Hibernation 17, 113, 124–125

Infrasound 39
Jellyfish 8–9, 28–29, 57, 61, 69, 86–87, 107
Kangaroo 66–67
Keratin 93, 95
Krill 40–41
Larva 29, 47, 61
Marsupial 66–67
Metamorphosis 61
Migration 110–111
Mimicry 88–89
Mole 108–109
Molting 26–27, 61
Moth 61, 71
Mucus 122–123
Octopus 97, 101
Opossum 83
Owl 23, 85
Oxygen 18–19, 65
Panda 54
Peacock 62
Pheromone 70–71
Polyp 29, 106–107
Porcupine 92–93
Porcupinefish 80–81
Rabbit 108–109
Ruminant 37

Sailfish 119
Shark 12–13, 39, 81, 113
Skunk 98–99
Sloth 17
Slug 122–123
Snake 26-27, 38, 42-43, 71, 73, 83, 89, 96
Spider 50–51, 63, 114–115
Squid 100–101
Starfish 20–21
Stonefish 85
Sunfish 57
Tapetum 22–23
Tarsier 76–77
Termite 104–105
Territory 45, 116–117
Turtle 95, 111
Ultrasound 39, 53, 76–77
Venom 51, 87, 97
Web 50–51
Whale 15, 39–41, 49, 78
Wolf 32–33
Woodpecker 44–45
Zebra 90–91